P9-CCX-849

A NOTE TO PARENTS ABOUT BEING LAZY

Being a parent should never be confused with being a servant. Waiting on children hand and foot only creates resentful parents and children void of self-motivation and resourcefulness. It also robs children of the delight and fulfillment that comes from personal accomplishment.

The purpose of this book is to teach children how to avoid being lazy by taking care of themselves, cleaning up after themselves, and helping others. In addition, it teaches children how to maintain a positive attitude about work. Reading and discussing this book with your child can also teach him or her how to respond when he or she is being unfairly inconvenienced by another person's laziness.

Helping children concentrate on the outcome of their work, rather than on how much effort it requires, is an important step in addressing laziness. Another important step is turning work into a more pleasurable experience. Acknowledging and/or rewarding accomplishments is also crucial to raising a child who "pulls his or her own weight" in the family and community.

A Children's Book About

BEING LAZY

Managing Editor: Ellen Klarberg
Copy Editor: Annette Gooch
Editorial Assistant: Lana Eberhard
Art Director: Jennifer Wiezel
Production Artist: Gail Miller
Illustration Designer: Bartholomew
Inking Artist: Micah Schwaberow
Coloring Artist: Susie Hornig
Lettering Artist: Linda Hanney
Typographer: Communication Graphics

Copyright ©1988 Joy Berry

No part of this book may be reproduced by any mechanical,
photographic or electronic process, or in the form of a
phonographic recording, nor may it be stored in a retrieval system,
transmitted, or otherwise be copied for public or private use
without the written permission of the publisher.

Printed in the U.S.A.

A Children's Book About

BEING LAZY

By Joy Berry

GROLIER
B O O K S

GROLIER BOOKS IS A DIVISION OF GROLIER ENTERPRISES, INC.

This book is about Sam and his sister Maggie.

Reading about Sam and Maggie can help you understand and deal with **being lazy.**

Have people ever asked you to do
something they could do themselves?

Has anyone refused to help you when you needed help?

Sometimes people might ask you to do something because they are too lazy to do it for themselves. Sometimes people might not help you because they are too lazy to help.

People who are not willing to work are being lazy.

When you are with someone who is lazy:

- How do you feel?
- What do you think?
- What do you do?

When you are with someone who is lazy:

- You might feel frustrated, angry, and resentful.
- You might feel that the person expects you to do all the work.
- You might not want to be around the person.

It is important to treat others the way you want to be treated. If you do not want other people to be lazy around you, you should not be lazy around them.

Try not to be lazy. Do not ask anyone to do anything for you that you can do for yourself. Get things for yourself whenever possible.

Try not to be lazy. Keep yourself clean. Bathe yourself. Wash and comb your hair. Brush your teeth. Dress yourself. Decide what clothes you are going to wear. Put them on yourself.

Try not to be lazy. Keep your room neat. Help keep your house neat. Put things away after you use them. Clean up any mess you make.

Try not to be lazy. Help out whenever you can. Here are some jobs you can do:

- Set the table for meals.
- Clean the table after meals.
- Help with the dishes.
- Empty the trash.

Taking care of yourself, cleaning up after yourself, or helping out might not always be easy. Sometimes these things take work.

Try to have a good attitude about your work.

- Do not complain about it.
- Do not wait to be reminded to do it.
- Do not try to get out of doing it.
- Do not put it off until later.

These things can make your work more fun:

- *Play this game with yourself.* Set a time limit and try to get the job done in that length of time. Be sure to give yourself enough time to do the job correctly.
- *Reward yourself.* Promise yourself you will do something you really enjoy after you finish your job. Be sure to keep the promise you make to yourself.

You help the people around you to be happy when you are not lazy. You also help yourself become a better person.